Ready, Set, Go Green!
Grades 2–3

Eco-Friendly Activities for Schoo'

By Teresa Domnauer

This product is printed on 100% recycled paper with soy ink! That means no trees were harmed in the making of this book. When you are finished with this book, please share it with a friend or recycle it.

Published by

Frank Schaffer
Publications®

Columbus, Ohio

Table of Contents

Writer: Teresa Domnauer
Editor: Lindsay Mizer
Design Lead: Joseph Giddings

Frank Schaffer Publications®

Send all inquiries to:
Frank Schaffer Publications
8720 Orion Place
Columbus, Ohio 43240-2111

ISBN: 0-7682-3573-1—*Ready, Set, Go Green! Grades 2–3*

1 2 3 4 5 6 7 8 PAT 12 11 10 09

Congratulations on choosing the best in educational materials from Frank Schaffer Publications. The *Ready, Set, Go Green!* series features activities that help students understand the value of our planet's resources. Students will also discover the many ways they can help protect the environment.

The *Ready, Set, Go Green!* books can be used at school or at home. Each book contains four sections on land, air, water, and plants and animals. In each section, you will find:

- **Face the Facts:** attention-grabbing factual information.
- **Ten Tips for School:** Eco-friendly tips for school.
- **Ten Tips for Home:** Eco-friendly tips for home.
- **Project Ideas:** A variety of fun project ideas.
- **Curriculum Connections:** Activities related to a variety of subject areas, including math, science, literature, writing, art, and more.
- **Activities:** Reproducible activity pages.
- **Reproducible Certificate:** A certificate of achievement to boost self-confidence.

At the end of the book, you will also find writing prompts, a checklist, a quiz, a glossary, and additional Internet resources.

This is the perfect series to help young learners understand the condition of our environment. It will encourage them to do something about it and to appreciate the value of Earth's natural resources.

So, get ready, get set...go green!

Sincerely,
Frank Schaffer Publications

Ready, Set, Go Green! Grades 2–3

Face the Facts

Millions of plastic bags become litter each year.

Every year, people throw away millions of books, magazines, and newspapers.

Americans use over 14 billion disposable Styrofoam™ coffee cups every year. These cups don't biodegrade either.

Nine out of ten plastic water bottles are thrown away rather than recycled. This results in millions of plastic bottles being tossed into landfills.

Plastic bags that are dumped into landfills will be there for hundreds of years. They don't biodegrade, or break down, into the Earth.

Just over 12 percent of landfills are made up of food scraps, most of which could be composted instead of thrown away.

Nearly 40 percent of the trash we throw away is paper. This paper could be recycled instead.

Paper mills are some of the biggest polluters in U.S. industry.

People in the United States throw away over 1.5 million writing pens every year.

Hundreds of thousands of CDs, DVDs, and batteries are thrown away each year.

Ready, Set, Go Green! Grades 2–3

Ten Tips for School: Land

1. Pick up litter on the playground and in the schoolyard. Be proud of your school and keep it clean!

2. Recycle as many paper products as you can.

3. Recycle aluminum cans and plastic bottles.

4. Be careful when you use art supplies. Don't spill or waste them.

5. Use both sides of a sheet of paper before recycling it.

6. Bring your lunch to school in a lunch box instead of a paper bag or other disposable bag.

7. Bring your food and drink in reusable containers, instead of ones you would throw away. For example, put your juice in a reusable plastic bottle instead of bringing a juice box.

8. Reuse recycled plastic containers from home for painting and other projects.

9. Recycle aluminum containers from hot lunches.

10. Share what you learn about "being green" with others—family members, classmates, and friends!

1. Think about how you can reuse things before automatically throwing them away.

2. Share and trade toys, books, and clothing with friends and family members.

3. Reuse wrapping paper and bows for gifts. Design your own wrapping paper from paper bags and old maps, too!

4. When you go to the grocery store, take reusable bags. That way, you don't have to get new ones each time. Find out if your grocery store recycles plastic bags.

5. Buy used clothing and toys instead of buying them new.

6. Wash and reuse re-sealable plastic food storage bags.

7. Find out what kinds of things your town or city recycles. Then, recycle as much as you can.

8. Make homemade cards and gifts instead of buying them. Or, send an e-card instead of buying a paper one.

9. Use rechargeable batteries instead of disposable ones.

10. Start a compost box for food scraps and yard waste.

Project Ideas: Land

Schools are usually gathering places in a community. Help encourage recycling in your community by starting a drop-off center at your school. Collect recyclable items and then take them to a recycling center.

Adopt a local park, stream, or beach. Visit it once a month and spend the day cleaning it up. Pick up litter and debris, empty trash cans, and paint benches.

Learn how to compost. Create a compost heap in an outdoor location or in a compost box. Use the compost to fertilize trees, plants, flowers, or a garden.

Electric products are a problem for the environment when they aren't recycled properly. Research to find out which electronic products are recyclable. Then, donate these items or collect them and e-cycle them.

Brainstorm a list of five new ways to use old things. For example, you can use a glass jar to make a bank or a plastic milk jug to make a bird feeder. Then, do them!

Put on a play about ways to help take care of the planet. Create costumes from recycled materials, such as paper bags, old clothes, and fabric scraps. Make posters to advertise the show, and then perform it for friends, neighbors, and family.

Spend some of your free time volunteering for an environmental cause. Go to the library or use the Internet to find an eco-friendly cause that you care about. Do what you can to help the cause.

Tell others that you care about the planet. Write an earth-friendly message on an old plain T-shirt. Wear it proudly.

Curriculum Connections: Land

 LITERATURE

Read *Follow That Trash!* by Francine Jacobs. Discuss the topics the author writes about in this book. Then, do a book report about it. Write about the main ideas in the story. Discuss what you liked and disliked about the book.

 Writing

Write a story about what you think life would be like in the year 2075 if people don't stop polluting the Earth. Then, write another story about what you think life would be like in the year 2075 if people stop polluting the Earth.

 Math

Use the topic of recycling to work on graphing and categorizing skills. Sort a group of recyclable materials into the correct bins. Then, graph the number of plastic, glass, paper, and aluminum items in each bin.

Science

Read and find out how worms help the soil and the environment. Then, make a worm box! Fill a large plastic bin with about six handfuls of topsoil. Make sure the box has sufficient air holes and drainage holes. Add compost worms. Then, add vegetable and fruit scraps on top of the worms. Cover the food scraps with strips of wet paper. Place the lid on the box and check the box every few days. Write about the results. Use the compost from the box around plants and trees.

Social Studies

Find out how other towns and cities across the nation recycle. Research and read about the "greenest" city in the U.S. What is this city like? What does it do differently than your town or city?

ART

Make a comic book with a story about recycling and keeping the planet clean. Invent a "green" superhero to star in the story.

Music

Write your own song about recycling. Use the tune of *Twinkle, Twinkle, Little Star* and come up with your own lyrics. Teach it to your friends and family members.

Physical Education

Go on a scavenger hunt in your favorite outdoor location. Make a list of items to look for in this spot and then go on a hike to find them. Check them off your list when you see them.

HEALTH

Visit the library or use the Internet to find out how some garbage causes health problems for humans.

What Does It Mean to Be "Green"?

Directions: Almost everyone talks about "being green" these days. What do you think it means to be green? Write your thoughts below.

Is It Biodegradable?

Something that is biodegradable breaks down easily—it then becomes part of nature again. Things like paper and yard waste are biodegradable. Things like plastic and aluminum are not.

Directions: Make a list of things that are biodegradable. Then, make a list of things that are not.

Biodegradable	Not Biodegradable
_____	_____
_____	_____
_____	_____
_____	_____
_____	_____
_____	_____
_____	_____
_____	_____
_____	_____
_____	_____

Ready, Set, Go Green! Grades 2–3

Name: _____

Practice the Three R's

Directions: If you practice the three R's, you can make less trash! Draw a picture of something that you could use less of, such as paper towels. Draw a picture of something that you could reuse, such as a cardboard box. Draw a picture of something that you could recycle, such as a plastic bottle.

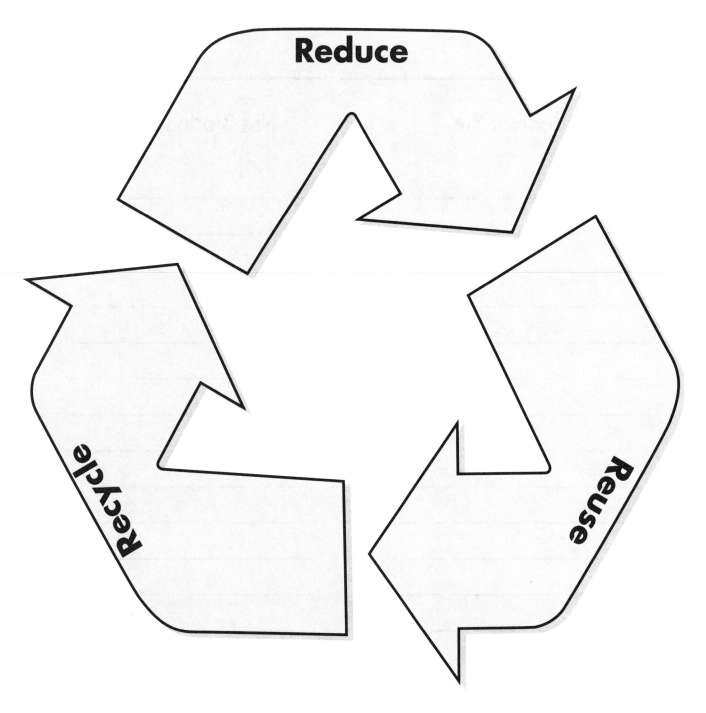

Ready, Set, Go Green! Grades 2–3

Recycling to the Max

Directions: Make a list of the things that you recycle at home. Then, check with your city or town to make sure that you are recycling everything that you possibly can. Hang the list on your refrigerator as a reminder.

Name: _____

My Special Spot

Directions: Think about your favorite place in nature. Draw a picture of it in the space below. Write a sentence to describe it. Now, imagine what this place would look like if it were filled with trash and pollution. Do your part to keep this from happening!

Certificate of
Green Achievement!

_____

has finished learning about land and the environment.

Congratulations for caring about our home, the Earth! Don't forget to share what you have learned with others.

Signed: _____

Date: _____

Face the Facts

As global warming continues, scientists predict there will be more heat waves, powerful hurricanes, and wildfires.

Compact fluorescent light bulbs use 60% less energy than regular light bulbs.

The United States emits 25 percent of the planet's greenhouse gases.

Every day, the Earth receives enough energy from sunlight to supply our energy needs for 4 or 5 years!

Microwave ovens are 3 to 4 times more energy efficient than electric ovens.

In the United States, we use over 8 million barrels of oil per day to fuel our cars. Burning gasoline fills the air with tons of carbon dioxide.

In Copenhagen, Denmark, hundreds of thousands of people bike to work each day instead of driving.

Because of global warming, glaciers all around the world are melting and disappearing.

Even when they are turned off, things like cell phone chargers, hair dryers, and televisions still use energy.

Each year, heating and cooling our homes creates 150 million tons of carbon dioxide emissions.

Ten Tips for School: Air

1. If adults are picking you up from school in a car, ask them not to leave the motor running while they wait for you.

2. Instead of having an adult drive you, ask permission to walk or ride your bicycle to school. Encourage your friends to do the same.

3. If you have to drive to school, try to carpool with friends and neighbors.

4. Ride the bus or other public transportation if you have to drive to school.

5. Make sure the classroom's computers and printers are turned off at the end of the day. Don't forget to turn off the monitors and speakers, too.

6. Turn off classroom lights when they are not in use and as much as you can.

7. Keep classroom shades up during the winter so the sun can warm the room. This keeps the heater from having to run as much.

8. Keep classroom shades down during the summer to block the sun's rays. This keeps the air conditioner from having to run as much.

9. Air pollution happens indoors, too! Whenever you can, open classroom windows to let in the fresh air.

10. Ask school staff to use energy saving light bulbs called *compact fluorescents*. They use a lot less electricity than regular light bulbs do.

Ten Tips for Home: Air

1. Instead of asking an adult to drive you, ride your bicycle or walk to the store, the park, or a friend's house.

2. Keep blinds and shades closed during the summer to block the sun's rays and keep the house cooler.

3. Ask your parent to buy locally grown fruits and vegetables. They require less fuel and energy to get to you!

4. Instead of turning up the heat, put on a sweater or put extra blankets on your bed.

5. Remind adults to try to use the air conditioner only when necessary.

6. Turn off and unplug any electronics in your room before you go to sleep each night.

7. Turn off lights when you aren't using them and each time you leave a room.

8. Hang clothes out to dry on a clothesline whenever possible, instead of using the clothes dryer.

9. Turn off the television if you are not watching it.

10. Play outside instead of watching TV!

Project Ideas: Air

Find out what factories and businesses in your town do to reduce air pollution. Have someone from the business come and talk to your class about their actions.

Research and find out how the Earth's ozone layer is thinning or disappearing in some areas. Make a list of five reasons why the disappearing ozone layer could be harmful for the Earth.

Trace your hand on a sheet of paper. On each finger, write one way that you can help stop air pollution.

Birds are creatures of the air. Help these animals build their nests! Place some simple nesting materials, such as yarn, grass clippings, and hair from your hairbrush, into a mesh bag. Place the bag outside and watch for nests that are filled with these materials.

Write a story about what would happen to people's health if we don't reduce air pollution. Share your story with friends, classmates, and family members.

Make a poster that gives people five ideas about how to save electricity. Hang the poster on your refrigerator or in a place where a lot of people will see it.

Wind power is a kind of power, or energy, which comes from wind. Windmills and wind turbines are used to collect this energy. Visit the library or use the Internet to find out where windmill and wind-turbine farms are located around the U.S. and the world.

Earth Day happens every year on April 22. On this day, people take time to think about the Earth. Plan a big Earth Day celebration for your family or for your classroom at school.

 LITERATURE

Read *Clean Air* by Rufus Bellamy. Discuss the topics the author writes about in this book. Then, do a book report about it. Write about the main ideas in the story. Discuss what you liked and disliked about the book.

 Writing

Research more about global warming. Write a report about what scientists think are its causes and effects. Write about the problems you think the Earth will encounter if the climate continues to get warmer.

 Math

Use the Internet to check the air quality index for your town or city each day for 30 days. Graph your findings.

Science

Research sources of clean energy, such as wind, solar, and hydropower. Write a report or create a computer presentation to share your findings.

Social Studies

Find out which cities throughout the world have the most air pollution. Locate the cities in an atlas or on a globe. Find out what causes them to have the most air pollution.

 ## ART

Make a kite and fly it on a windy day.

 ## Music

Come up with a song that will encourage people to stop polluting the air. Write lyrics to the song and title it "Clean Air for Everyone."

 ## Physical Education

Work in your yard or garden or volunteer to help a neighbor. It's a great way to get fresh air and exercise!

 ## HEALTH

Visit the library or use the Internet to learn about the different causes of air pollution and how it affects our health.

Fabulous Fresh Air!

Directions: Imagine that you are walking outside on a cool, windy day. Close your eyes and imagine how it feels and smells to breathe in the fresh air. Write a list of words to describe how you feel. Then, use your word list to write a poem about fresh, clean air.

_____   _____

_____   _____

_____   _____

_____   _____

_____   _____

_____   _____

Title: _____

_____

_____

_____

_____

_____

_____

_____

_____

_____

_____

_____

_____

Get Moving Without Polluting!

Directions: There are many ways to travel from place to place. Some forms of transportation cause air pollution, and some do not. The vehicles in the word box do not cause air pollution. Find them in the puzzle. The words go across and down.

Word Box

bicycle	scooter	roller skates	sailboat
skateboard	canoe	kayak	

```
L  E  T  P  R  I  E  A  Z  N  P  T  O
F  G  O  O  R  P  K  A  Y  A  K  S  S
A  M  A  S  T  R  O  N  O  M  E  C  A
E  B  I  C  Y  C  L  E  O  Z  C  O  I
A  X  R  S  P  D  O  K  D  O  I  O  L
F  W  L  C  N  U  Z  N  W  H  P  T  B
C  U  I  E  Y  C  S  M  E  B  I  E  O
E  J  I  C  S  C  T  T  B  G  T  R  A
S  K  A  T  E  B  O  A  R  D  A  J  T
O  T  Q  E  W  S  E  A  V  C  T  U  D
I  R  O  L  L  E  R  S  K  A  T  E  S
M  O  Y  V  P  R  I  D  A  H  O  R  S
A  P  E  H  I  C  A  N  O  E  N  I  E
```

Ready, Set, Go Green! Grades 2–3

Green Fun

If you use less electricity, you make less air pollution. That is because we have to burn fuels to make electricity, and these fuels pollute the air.

Directions: You can save electricity by choosing activities that don't use electricity. Make a list of green activities that you will do this week.

SUNDAY	
MONDAY	
TUESDAY	
WEDNESDAY	
THURSDAY	
FRIDAY	
SATURDAY	

A Clean, Green Car

Solar, wind, and water power (hydroelectric power) do not cause air pollution. These kinds of clean power are called *renewable energy sources*. They give people other ways to make electricity.

Directions: Design a car for the future that is powered by a renewable energy source. Label the car with captions to explain how it works.

Name: _____

I Promise...

Directions: Remember, using less electricity makes less air pollution. What are some ways that you can pledge to save electricity? Write them below.

I promise to...

_____

_____

_____

_____

_____

_____

_____

_____

_____

_____

Certificate of
Green Achievement!

_____

has finished learning about air and the environment.

Congratulations for caring about our home, the Earth! Don't forget to share what you have learned with others.

Signed: _____

Date: _____

Face the Facts

As a result of global warming, scientists believe there will be less rainwater and more droughts.

Lake Chad in Africa used to be the world's 6th biggest lake. Global warming has caused it to shrink to 1/20th of its size!

We can save thousands of gallons of water each year by running the dishwasher only when it is full.

Nearly half of the water supplied to homes is flushed down the toilet.

Hydropower, or water power, delivers 20 percent of the world's electricity.

Homes with leaky faucets can waste 90 gallons of water per day.

If a family uses a water-saving showerhead, they can save thousands of gallons of water each year!

A family can also save thousands of gallons of water each year if the members take shorter showers.

Scientists believe that global warming may eventually cause the Earth's sea levels to rise, flooding many coastal cities.

Americans use billions of gallons of water each year, just for watering their lawns.

33

Ready, Set, Go Green! Grades 2–3

Ten Tips for School: Water

1. When you need to wash your hands, do it quickly and in cold water. Don't let the water run for too long!

2. Collect water in rain barrels and use it to water your school's plants, flowers, or vegetable garden.

3. Encourage your school staff to use environmentally friendly soaps and cleaning products.

4. Use environmentally friendly cleaning products in your classroom.

5. Find out how to properly dispose of paints and other hazardous waste.

6. Remember that whatever you put down the sink drain or flush down the toilet goes back into our drinking water supply.

7. Collect materials from classroom projects and wash them all at one time.

8. Dripping faucets waste water. Make sure all faucets are turned off completely when you are done using them.

9. Pick up trash from around your school building so that it doesn't flow into sewers.

10. Whenever you use the tap, don't turn it on full force. This saves water.

Ten Tips for Home: Water

1. Turn off the faucet while you are brushing your teeth and anytime that you are not actually using the water.

2. Remember, whatever you pour down the sink drain will end up in our water supply!

3. Remind your parents to wash only full loads of laundry and to use cold water.

4. Collect water in a rain barrel in your backyard. You can use the collected water for your lawn and garden.

5. Water lawns and gardens early in the morning or in the evening, before the sun comes up or after the sun has gone down.

6. Help your family replace parts of your lawn with a rock garden or with plants native to your area. They don't need as much water as lawns do.

7. Ask a parent to help you find recipes for household cleaners made from nontoxic ingredients, such as white vinegar, baking soda, and lemon juice.

8. Make sure the dishwasher is full before turning it on.

9. Wash your hands quickly and in cold water.

10. Always clean up after your pet. Pet waste can lead to contamination of water.

Project Ideas: Water

Visit the library or use the Internet to learn more about animals that live in the water. The Web site for the Monterey Bay Aquarium in California is a great place to start. (http://mbayaq.org/)

Have a fundraiser, such as a tag sale or a bake sale, and donate the proceeds to an organization that protects water habitats.

Take a field trip to a water treatment facility in your town. Learn how our water is treated before it comes through our faucets to use.

Invite a representative from your local water department to come and speak to your classroom about conserving water. Brainstorm a list of questions to ask the representative before he or she comes.

Write a letter to your state senator, governor, or city leader. Tell him or her about your concerns about a water pollution related issue. The Natural Resources Defense Council's Earth Action Web site can help you. (http://www.nrdc.org/action/default.asp)

Create a wall mural of an ocean scene. Draw pictures of animals and plants that live in the ocean. Then, add pictures of things that pollute the ocean. Add captions to label your pictures.

Visit the Natural Resources Defense Council's Make Waves Web site, titled "How Kids Can Protect the Earth One Ripple at a Time." (http://www.nrdc.org/makewaves/) Learn how you can prevent water pollution.

Take a field trip to a waterfowl preserve. Write a report about one of the animals you see there.

Curriculum Connections: Water

 LITERATURE

Read *One Well: The Story of Water on Earth* by Rochelle Strauss. Discuss the topics the author writes about in this book. Then, do a book report about it. Write about the main ideas in the story. Discuss what you liked and disliked about the book.

 **Writing**

Write a story about an endangered animal that lives in a water habitat. Research to find information about this animal and its watery home. When you finish the story, share it with classmates and friends.

 Math

Choose ten American cities and find out the average rainfall for each city. Then, graph your findings and discuss the results.

 Science

Study the water cycle and create a poster that illustrates each part of the cycle.

Social Studies

Find out where the nearest water habitat is in your town or city. Locate the site on a map and find out what kinds of plants and animals live there. Visit the water habitat if you can.

ART

Use watercolors to create a painting of a water habitat, such as an ocean, river, or stream. Be sure to include all of the plants and animals of this habitat in your painting.

Music

Write a song that tells people how polluted water harms people and animals. Use a familiar tune, such as *Row, Row, Row Your Boat.*

Physical Education

Enjoy some time in the water! Go for a swim at a local pool, lake, or beach. Swimming is great exercise.

HEALTH

Why is drinking water so important to your health? Brainstorm the reasons why you think drinking water is important. Then, research to find out the real health benefits of drinking water and see if you were correct.

How We Use Water

Directions: Inside each water droplet, write a way that people and animals use water every day.

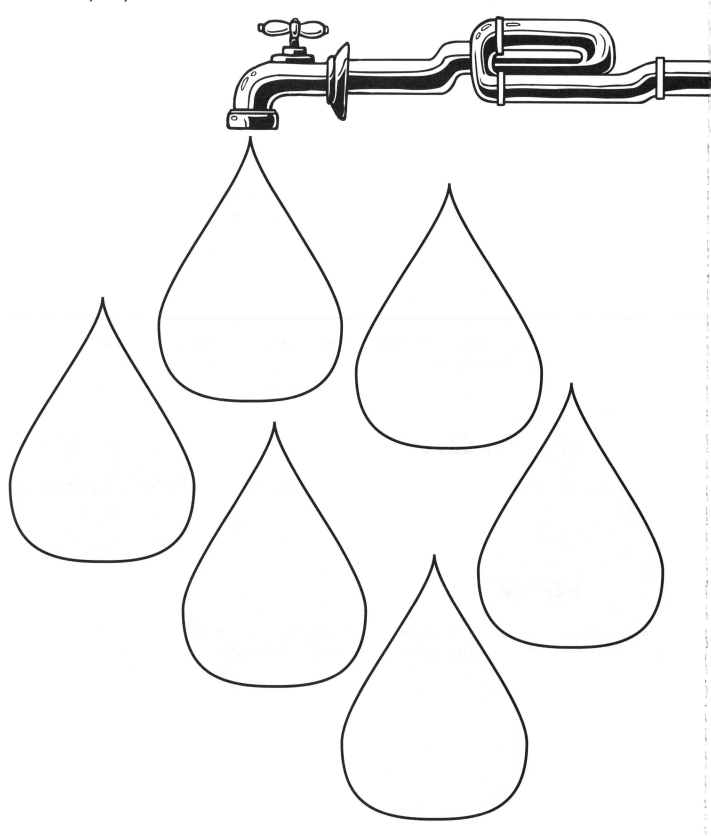

Water Habitats

It is important that we do not pollute water habitats. These habitats are some animals' homes!

Directions: Make a list of animals and plants that live in each water habitat below.

Ocean	River	Pond
_____	_____	_____
_____	_____	_____
_____	_____	_____
_____	_____	_____
_____	_____	_____
_____	_____	_____
_____	_____	_____
_____	_____	_____

Name: _____

How I Can Save Water

Directions: Make a list of the ways that you can save water in each room below.

Bathroom	Kitchen	Laundry Room
_____	_____	_____
_____	_____	_____
_____	_____	_____
_____	_____	_____
_____	_____	_____
_____	_____	_____
_____	_____	_____
_____	_____	_____
_____	_____	_____

Ready, Set, Go Green! Grades 2–3

Melting Glaciers

Directions: A glacier is a huge river of ice that moves slowly. The Earth's warmer temperatures are causing glaciers in the Arctic to melt! Why do you think this might cause problems? Write your ideas below.

_____

_____

_____

_____

_____

_____

_____

_____

_____

_____

_____

_____

Water Power

Directions: Hydropower is power, or energy, that comes from moving water. This form of energy does not cause pollution to the Earth. One way that scientists get hydropower is from dams. Research the pros and cons of this form of hydropower. Write them below.

Pros ☺	_____ _____ _____ _____ _____ _____
Cons ☹	_____ _____ _____ _____ _____

Certificate of
Green Achievement!

_____

has finished learning about water and the environment.

Congratulations for caring about our home, the Earth! Don't forget to share what you have learned with others.

Signed: _____

Date: _____

Face the Facts

Making recycled paper requires a lot less energy—70 to 90 percent less—than it does to make new paper. It also protects forests!

At one time, southern white rhinoceroses were thought to be extinct. Thanks to careful protection, these animals are now the only rhinos listed as non-endangered!

Hundreds of thousands of trees are chopped down each year to make paper for books.

Global warming could cause hundreds of thousands of species to become extinct within the next 50 years.

Trees take in carbon dioxide, a greenhouse gas. One tree can absorb 2,000 pounds of carbon dioxide during its lifetime. This helps stop global warming.

Even though they have been protected for many years, seven kinds of great whales are still endangered.

Millions of trees are cut down each year for mills that make paper and paper products.

Scientists believe that there are only about 700 mountain gorillas left in the wild in central Africa.

There are about 3,000 manatees left in the United States. Many manatee deaths are caused by human behavior.

Rain forests create a large amount of the planet's oxygen and contain over half of the world's wildlife. But these amazing forests are getting smaller and smaller every day!

Ready, Set, Go Green! Grades 2–3

Ten Tips for School: Plants and Animals

1. Take care of classroom supplies so they last a long time and the school doesn't have to buy new ones. Buying new stuff uses energy and natural resources!

2. Grow lots of plants in the classroom. Plants take in carbon dioxide and give off oxygen, slowing global warming.

3. Sponsor an endangered animal.

4. Instead of buying new books and magazines, check them out from the library instead. This saves precious trees!

5. When working on the computer, print only the pages you are absolutely sure you need and will use.

6. If you have to buy a book, try to buy it used.

7. Bring in junk mail or used paper from home to use as scrap paper in the classroom.

8. Plant a tree, an herb garden, a flower garden, or even a vegetable garden in your schoolyard.

9. Bring in your old magazines and books to share with classmates.

10. Buy school supplies in bulk—it uses less packaging materials.

Ten Tips for Home: Plants and Animals

1. Plant a tree in your backyard. Or grow your own vegetables and flowers. If you don't have a backyard, you can plant seeds in pots or containers.

2. Sponsor an endangered animal.

3. Cut up the plastic holders from six-packs of soda before throwing them away. This keeps birds and other animals from getting tangled up in them.

4. If you are hiking, pick up any trash you see along the trail. This will help protect the forest habitat, which is home to many plants and animals. Remember, don't leave anything behind, even food scraps.

5. Save valuable trees by reducing the amount of paper products you use. For example, use washable cloths for cleaning and spills instead of paper towels. Avoid using paper plates whenever possible. Send e-cards instead of buying paper ones!

6. Rent movies and video games instead of buying them new at the store.

7. Need a gift for someone? Purchase a tree to be planted in honor of that person at www.americanforests.org.

8. Use cloth napkins instead of paper napkins. You'll save trees!

9. Bring reusable bags to the grocery store. You'll save trees and keep plastic bags out of the landfills.

10. Try to buy items that are recycled and have the least packaging. If you buy something small at a store, say "no" to the bag and carry it instead.

Ready, Set, Go Green! Grades 2–3

Project Ideas: Plants and Animals

Take good care of your textbooks so that your school doesn't have to buy new ones. This will save trees! Make covers for all of your books out of old paper bags, wrapping paper, newspapers, or maps.

Research and make a list of ten interesting facts about an endangered animal. Share your list with your friends and family members. Find out what you can do to help this endangered animal.

Put on a skit about endangered animals. Make costumes from recycled materials, such as scrap paper, fabric, and paper bags.

Plants help stop global warming! They take in carbon dioxide and give off oxygen. Do your part and plant a tree or flowers at home or at school.

Find out how to make handmade paper, using junk mail and old paper scraps for pulp. Use your handmade paper to make cards and invitations, instead of buying new ones.

Make a classroom tree! Draw the outline of a tree on a wall in your classroom. Make paper leaves for the tree. On each leaf, write a way in which you can help save the planet and its endangered animals.

Research rain forests and find out how we use the many different kinds of trees and plants that grow there.

Find out what kinds of trees and plants are native to your area. Find out what kinds of fruits, vegetables, and nuts are grown in your area. If you don't have any of these plants in your yard, plant them! They typically need less watering and care than nonnative plants.

Curriculum Connections: Plants and Animals

 LITERATURE

Read *The Lorax* by Dr. Seuss. Discuss the topics the author writes about in this book. Then, do a book report about it. Write about the main ideas in the story. Discuss what you liked and disliked about the book.

 Writing

Write an essay about the rain forest. Research and find out more about it. Be sure to include information on its inhabitants, location, and the valuable things it provides to us.

 **Math**

Make up your own story problems that include plants and animals. The problems can include addition, subtraction, multiplication, or division. Share the problems with a friend to see if he or she can solve them.

 Science

Plant a butterfly bush and observe its visitors. Visit the library or use the Internet to find out what kinds of butterflies inhabit your area.

Social Studies

Learn about the plants and animals that live in your region and determine what type of biome you live in. How does the biome you live in differ from the other biomes on Earth?

 ## ART

Take a walk outside and sketch the plants and animals you see. Use the sketch to create a watercolor painting or a pastel drawing.

 ## Music

Write song lyrics that begin with "We share the planet with…"

 ## Physical Education

Go on a nature hike and take a quiet moment to observe the plants and animals around you.

 ## HEALTH

Research how to grow your own organic fruits and vegetables. Then, try it. Organic produce is great for your health!

Endangered Animals Word Scramble

Directions: Unscramble the words to find the names of endangered animals. Write the animals' names on the lines.

1. tinag andap _____

2. ralpo rabe _____

3. riteg _____

4. cosoerrihn _____

5. antphele _____

6. lube lawhe _____

7. lalgroi _____

8. rainme letutr _____

Endangered Animal Poem

Directions: Use this page to write a poem about an endangered animal. Write the name of the animal vertically on the page. Each line should begin with the letter at the beginning of the line.

____ _____

____ _____

____ _____

____ _____

____ _____

____ _____

____ _____

____ _____

Green House

Directions: This house needs some green! Use crayons or markers to add colorful trees, plants, and flowers to the yard of this house. Then, write a short paragraph explaining how green plants and trees are good for the environment.

_____

_____

_____

_____

_____

Rain Forest Friends

Directions: Visit the library or use the Internet to find out what kinds of animals live in the rain forest. Draw them below.

Gifts From the Earth

Directions: People use many natural resources from the Earth. We use trees to make homes and furniture, plants to make medicines, and oil to fuel our cars. What other gifts does the Earth give us? Write a list of your ideas below.

1. _____
2. _____
3. _____
4. _____
5. _____
6. _____
7. _____
8. _____
9. _____
10. _____

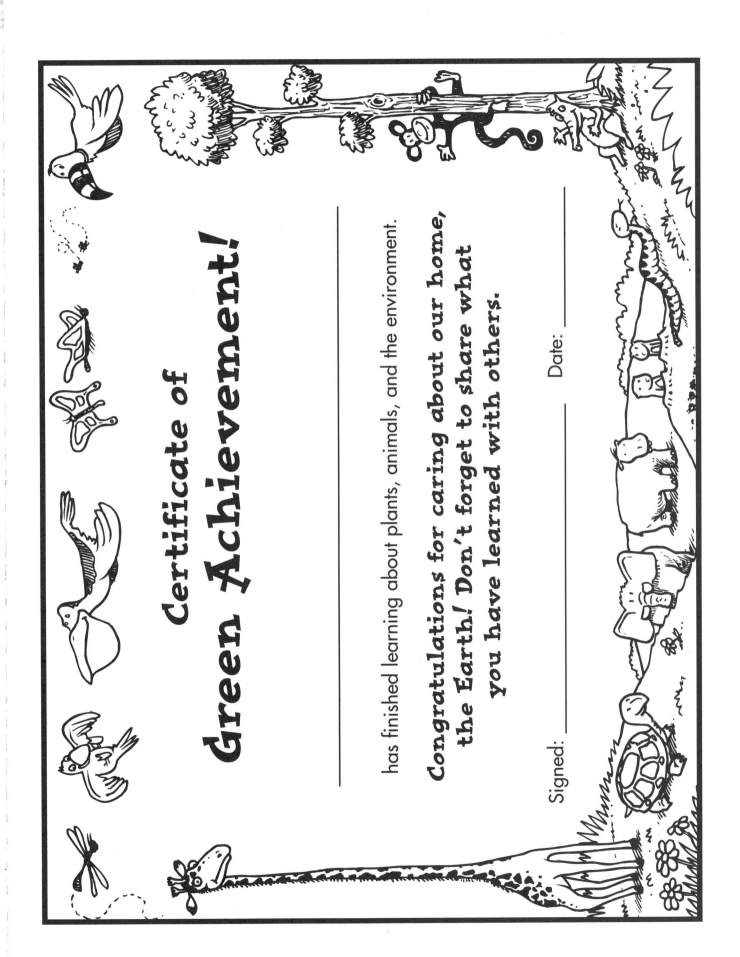

Certificate of
Green Achievement!

_____

has finished learning about plants, animals, and the environment.

Congratulations for caring about our home, the Earth! Don't forget to share what you have learned with others.

Signed: _____

Date: _____

Write About It

Below are some ideas to get you thinking about being green. Read each prompt and then write about it.

Taking care of the planet is important to me because...

I can help the planet by...

I want to help protect endangered animals because...

I can save electricity by...

I can reduce how much trash I make by...

I can use less water by...

Pollution hurts people because...

My favorite outdoor place is...

Nature is special to me because...

My hope for planet Earth is...

Green Checklist

Here are ways that I can help the planet:

☐

☐

☐

☐

☐

☐

☐

☐

☐

☐

☐

☐

☐

Ready, Set, Go Green! Grades 2–3

Green Quiz

Name: _____

1. What are the three R's?

_____   _____   _____

2. What kinds of power do not cause air pollution?

_____

3. List four endangered animals.

_____

4. What are three ways to save water?

_____

_____

_____

5. What is a landfill?

_____

6. What two words make up the word *smog*?

_____   _____

7. What do we call the protective layer of air around the Earth?

_____

8. What do scientists call the warming of Earth's climate?

_____

9. What kinds of items can you recycle?

_____

10. What does the word *biodegradable* mean?

_____

Green Glossary

biodegradable: describes a substance that breaks down easily

clean energy: energy that does not cause pollution

endangered: at risk of becoming extinct

global warming: the gradual warming of Earth's climate

greenhouse gases: harmful gases that trap heat around the Earth

hydropower: power, or energy, created by moving water

landfill: a place where trash is dumped

natural resources: things that come from the Earth, such as trees, oil, and minerals

ozone layer: the protective layer of air around the Earth

pollute: to make dirty in an unhealthy way

reduce: to use less of

reuse: to use again

recycle: to make new again

smog: harmful air pollutant made of smoke and fog

Answer Key for Green Quiz

1. reduce, reuse, recycle.
2. Answers vary. Examples include: solar, wind, or water power.
3. Answers vary. Examples include: mountain gorilla, black rhinoceros, marine turtle, chimpanzee, giant panda.
4. Answers vary. Examples include: taking shorter showers, washing hands quickly in cold water, turning water off while brushing teeth.
5. A place where trash is dumped.
6. Smoke and fog.
7. The ozone layer.
8. Global warming.
9. Answers vary. Examples include: paper, plastic, glass, and aluminum.
10. Describes something that breaks down easily.

Additional Internet Resources

Environmental Protection Agency Educational Resources
http://www.epa.gov/epahome/educational.htm

U.S. Department of Energy
Energy Efficiency and Renewable Energy, K–12 Lesson Plans
http://www.eere.energy.gov/education/lessonplans/

World Wildlife Fund
Features information about endangered species including giant pandas.
http://www.worldwildlife.org/species/index.html

Animal Planet's Endangered Species Guide
http://animal.discovery.com/guides/endangered/endangered.html

Solar Energy International
Kids' Info
http://www.solarenergy.org/resources/youngkids.html

Natural Resources Defense Council Earth Action Center
Site helps citizens stay informed about environmental issues and contact government officials.
http://www.nrdc.org/action/default.asp

Air Now
Information and activities for young people about air quality and air pollution.
http://airnow.gov/index.cfm?action=aqikids_new.main

The EPA's climate change kids' site:
http://www.epa.gov/climatechange/kids/

Nike Grind
http://www.nikebiz.com/responsibility/community_programs/reuse_a_shoe.html

Keep America Beautiful Kids' Zone
http://www.cleansweepusa.org/